THE HOLY ROSARY OF
THE BLESSED VIRGIN MARY
GOD'S PLAN

SANDRA P. ABRAMS

ISBN-13: 978-0615622903 (Abrams Family Publishing)

ISBN-10: 0615622909

Library of Congress Control Number: LCCN: 2012906239

Abrams Family Publishing, Murfreesboro, Tennessee

New American Bible Copyright 1992, 1987, 1980, 1970 by Catholic Book Publishing CO, New York, N.Y. Printed in the United States of America.

Acknowledgements

I thank God for the beautiful gifts He has given me.

A special thanks to my Loving husband William and our beautiful children for their patience and support throughout this beautiful project.

I also thank my Mother and my Aunt Isabel whom inspired me by planting seeds of Faith and Love.

Special thanks to all my friends and family for their input and advice.

Finally, I want to thank my Father because I know from heaven he enlightened me to go forward with this mission.

INTRODUCTION

The purpose of this book is to encourage every one of all ages to pray the Holy Rosary. The whole family and communities united in prayer will achieve peace in our hearts and have a better world.

By praying the Rosary we meditate on the most important moments in the life of Our Lord Jesus Christ and the Blessed Virgin Mary. Through the artwork depicting the mysteries, we feel penetrated with the infinite love that God gives to us every moment of our lives.

The Holy Rosary is the perfect connection of God the Father, God the Son and God the Holy Spirit by making it a holy moment worthy of worship and devotion. Thanks to the Blessed Virgin Mary who has taught us that the Rosary is our defense against the enemy, also gives us refuge and shelter for the relief of our sorrows and needs.

The Blessed Virgin Mary is always willing to be our advocate who tells us to pray without haste, meditate on each mystery, and absorb the teachings of Jesus. She calls us to conversion and to live our lives serving the Lord and mankind.

Pope John Paul II said to the faithful in St. Peter's Square, "The Rosary is my favorite prayer, is a ladder to climb to heaven."

To pray in unity is blessed. Jesus said, "I say to you, if two of you agree on earth about anything for which they are to pray, it shall be granted to them by my heavenly Father. For where two or three are gathered together in my name, there am I in the midst of them."
St Matthew 18: 19-20

All the wonders of this world are part of GOD'S PLAN. God gave us the Holy Rosary as a way to open our hearts and the door to the divine light. Feel the inner strength and peace as well as passionate love that make our prayers the most beautiful encounter with Him in our lives. That is why the end of the Rosary will give us a deep spiritual relationship with Him.

I hope you enjoy this book. When praying the Holy Rosary, pray in a quiet place and follow the beads and numbers in each mystery. Every day you can open up your creativity and motivate everybody with enthusiasm.

Thanks for following the request of the Blessed Virgin Mary, "Pray the Holy Rosary."

Sandra P. Abrams

JOYFUL MYSTERIES

★

To meditate on
the Joyful Mysteries as
indicated by their word is to
fully enjoy the events and to
feel how wonderful God is. He
gave us his Son, our Savior for
the forgiveness of our sins.

The Blessed Virgin Mary
was worthy of achieving this
promise to be the Mother of the
Son of God. She did not hesitate
to say a YES, I accept God's will.

For every Christian,
the Blessed Virgin Mary is
an admirable and honorable
presence in our lives as this
beautiful woman who brought
humility and virtues that
made her a wonderful mother.
She was especially worthy of
being nothing less than the
mother Jesus who would
give His life for us.

We also see the power of
God in this mystery. He gave
Zacharias and his wife a son
at a mature age. That child
opened the way for Jesus.

Observe how the angels obey
and serve as messengers for God.
Those who receive these messages
manifest the Glory of God the Father,
as in the case of the shepherds and
the Magi from the east who never
doubted the coming of
the Son of God.

LUMINOUS MYSTERIES

★

THE BIBLE

Behold the greatness of God's divine light by sending the Holy Spirit, who is constantly manifested in the life of Jesus. Others were converted in the Baptism of the Son of God and through his preaching and annunciation into the Kingdom of Heaven.

At the wedding Feast at Cana his disciples began to believe in him.
Jesus himself taught us through parables and miracles.

The appearance of Moses and Elijah on the mountain after the Transfiguration of Jesus makes us see a bit more of that great mystery and grandeur that contains Almighty God.

In this mystery we can note with perfection the meaning and love of God the Father in the sacrifice of giving the life of his beloved Son for the redemption of our sins. Every time we take the Eucharist, we remember that special moment for humanity. We know that each time we sin we offend Jesus. We are not worthy to receive the body of the Lord, but God is love.

SORROWFUL MYSTERIES

★

The most painful thing in a mother's life is when sees her son killed. The Blessed Virgin Mary had grief that was so deep. Her grief feels like sword in your heart.

The immense pain that Jesus felt was humiliating. The physical pain does not exceed the pain He felt when He saw men do evil.

This entire passion of Jesus portrays the kind of pain we feel when a friend betrays us, We live in aworld of injustices that we sometimes cannot withstand. We are often offended by prejudices and social conditions, but the saddest part is that we still hurt Jesus with our offenses.

GLORIOUS MYSTERIES

★

Contemplating the life of Jesus, Christians give glory to Him
by obeying His teachings, and mediating on His passion, crucifixion,
death and resurrection. With this we find the reasons for our own
Catholic Faith. Daily we find the Glory of our Lord Jesus Christ
in every step we take. In every experience we notice that the
words and teachings of the Gospel in all situations that we
have. We find the answers and solutions for our
situations through Jesus.

We glorify the Holy Trinity when we respect and fear God,
when we defend our faith, when we have faith, and when
we are patient with God's plans.

We glorify the Most Holy Trinity when we promote peace
within ourselves, have compassion for the needy, when we
obey God's commandments, and fulfill His divine messages.

We glorify him when we attend Holy Mass, participate in
the Holy Eucharist, and give witness to the Gospel.

Give glory in the unity of prayer, love to God, to
ourselves, and to all those around us so,
"They all be one in truth and charity."

The Sign of the Cross

1 ★
**In the name
of
the Father**

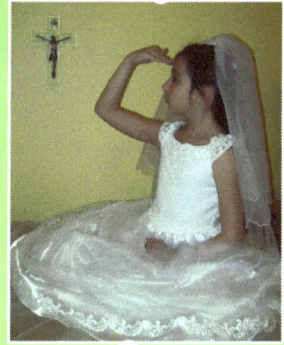

2 ★
**And of
the Son**

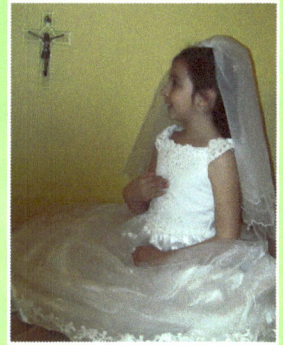

3 ★
**And of
the Holy**

★ **5**
Amen

4 ★
Spirit

THE APOSTLES' CREED

★

5 ★
And is Seated at the right hand of God, the Father Almighty; from there will come to judge the living and the dead.

4 ★
On the third day He rose again from the dead;

He ascended into heaven,

3 ★
Suffered under Pontius Pilate; was crucified, died and was buried; He descended into hell;

1 ★
I Believe in God, the Father Almighty, Creator of heaven and earth.

And in Jesus Christ, his only Son, our Lord,

2 ★
Who was conceived by the Holy Spirit, born of the Virgin Mary,

6 ★
I believe in the Holy Spirit,

7 ★
The Holy Catholic Church,

8 ★
The communion of Saints,

9 ★
The forgiveness of sins,

10 ★
The resurrection of the body and life everlasting.
★*Amen.*

1★ ACT OF CONTRITION

My God, I am sorry for
my sins with all my heart.

In choosing to do wrong
and falling to do good, I have sinned
against you whom I should love above
all things I firmly intend, with your help,
to do penance, to sin no more, and to
avoid whatever leads me to sin.

Our Savior Jesus Christ suffered and
died for us. In his name,
my God, have mercy.
★Amen.

2★

O God, whose only begotten Son,
by His life, death, and resurrection,
has purchased for us the rewards
of eternal salvation.

Grant, we beseech Thee, that while
meditating on these mysteries of
the most holy Rosary of the Blessed
Virgin Mary, that we may both
imitate what they contain and
obtain what they promise,
through Christ our Lord.
★Amen.

3★

My God, I believe, I adore,
I hope, and I love you.

I beg pardon of you for those,
who do not believe, do not adore,
do not hope, and do not love you.
★Amen

INTENTIONS

1

Lord, we humbly pray for you in Obedience of your Commandments and keep us united in constant prayer and worship to increase our faith.

2

Lord, teach us to be more tolerant and open to forgiveness. Give us the strength to responsibly defend our principles with humility.

3

Lord, give us the instruments that we need to build paths of peace and love to grow spiritually.

4

Lord, give us the compassion to exercise charity to help those in need.

5

Lord, we offer this Rosary for all sinners and the following personal intentions...

6

Lord, we thank you for all the blessings and love you give us each and every day.
Amen...

OUR FATHER

★

Our Father,

Who art in heaven,

Hallowed be Thy Name;

Thy Kingdom come;

Thy will be done,

on earth as it is

in Heaven.

★ Give us this day
our daily bread.

And forgive us
our trespasses,

as we forgive
those who trespass
against us.

And lead us not
into temptation,

but deliver us
from evil.

★ Amen.

1
HAIL MARY, BY VIRTUE OF FAITH

Hail Mary, full of grace,
the Lord is with thee; Blessed
art thou among women, and
blessed is the fruit of
thy womb, Jesus.

Holy Mary, Mother of God,
Pray for us sinners,
now and at the hour
of death.
Amen.

2
HAIL MARY, BY VIRTUE OF HOPE
Hail Mary..

3
HAIL MARY, BY VIRTUE OF CHARITY
Hail Mary..

4
Glory Be

Glory be to the Father,
and to the Son,
and to the Holy Spirit.

As it was in the beginning,
is now, and ever shall be,
world without end.
Amen.

THE JOYFUL MYSTERIES
Monday & Saturday

★

1st Joyful Mystery

The Annunciation of the Angel Gabriel to the Blessed Virgin Mary

★Our Father...

5★
Mary was engaged to a man named Joseph, from the house of David.
★Hail Mary...

4★
Mary was constantly in prayer and communication with God.
★Hail Mary...

3★
Mary was presented in the Temple, where she was devoted to God.
★Hail Mary...

1★
Joachim was deeply proud and loved his daughter Mary for her great virtues.
★Hail Mary...

2★
Anne admired her daughter Mary's Godly grace and wisdom.
★Hail Mary...

6★
The Angel Gabriel announced to Mary, "Hail, favored one! The Lord is with you."
★*Hail Mary...*

7★
Mary said, "Behold, I am the handmaid of the Lord. May it be done to me according to your word."
★*Hail Mary...*

12★
O My Jesus, forgive us our sins, save us from the fires of hell; lead all souls to heaven, especially those who are in most need of Thy mercy.
★*Amen.*

11★
Glory be to the Father, and to the Son and to the Holy Spirit.
★*As it was in the beginning, is now, and ever shall be, world without end.*
★*Amen.*

8★
An Angel told Joseph, "For it is through the Holy Spirit that this child has been conceived in her"
★*Hail Mary...*

9★
They shall name Him Jesus (Emmanuel), which means "God is with us".
★*Hail Mary...*

10★
The Holy Family of Nazareth: Jesus, Mary and Joseph.
★*Hail Mary...*

THE JOYFUL MYSTERIES
Monday & Saturday

★

2nd Joyful Mystery

The Blessed Virgin Mary Visits her cousin Elizabeth

★Our Father...

5★
Elizabeth said to Mary, "Most blessed are you among women, and blessed is the fruit of your womb."
★Hail Mary...

4★
When Elizabeth heard Mary's greeting, the infant leaped in her womb, and Elizabeth, filled with the Holy Spirit.
★Hail Mary...

3★
Mary traveled through to the hill country to the town of Judah; she visited her cousin Elizabeth.
★Hail Mary...

1★
The angel of the Lord announced to Zechariah, "Your wife Elizabeth will bear you a son, and you shall name him John."
★Hail Mary...

2★
John, will be great in the sight of the Lord.
★Hail Mary...

6★
Elizabeth said, "Blessed are you who believed that what was spoken to you by the Lord would be fulfilled."
★*Hail Mary...*

7★
Mary said, "My soul proclaims the greatness of the Lord; my spirit rejoices in God my Savior."
★*Hail Mary...*

12★
O My Jesus, forgive us our sins, save us from the fires of hell; lead all souls to heaven, especially those who are in most need of Thy mercy.
★*Amen.*

8★
The mighty one has done great things for me, and Holy is His name!
★*Hail Mary...*

11★
Glory be to the Father, and to the Son and to the Holy Spirit.
★*As it was in the beginning, is now, and ever shall be, world without end.*
★*Amen.*

9★
Mary and Joseph heard and obeyed God's messages through the Angel.
★*Hail Mary...*

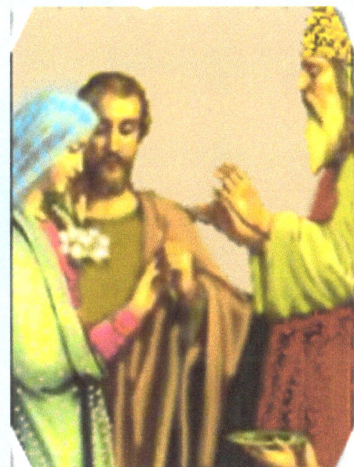

10★
All generations will call Mary, "Blessed."
★*Hail Mary...*

THE JOYFUL MYSTERIES
Monday & Saturday

★

3rd Joyful Mystery

The Nativity of the Divine Child Jesus in a Manger at Bethlehem

★*Our Father...*

5★
The three Magi from the East followed the star that took them to the newborn Jesus.
★*Hail Mary...*

4★
They stayed in a manger, where animals were sheltered.
★*Hail Mary...*

3★
When the time of delivery came; there was no room for them at the inn.
★*Hail Mary...*

1★
Joseph and Mary traveled from Nazareth to Bethlehem.
★*Hail Mary...*

2★
Joseph and Mary started looking for a place to stay after registering for the census.
★*Hail Mary...*

6★
The Angel announced to the shepherds, "In the city of David a Savior has been born to you who is Messiah and Lord."
★Hail Mary...

7★
The Angel said, "You will find an infant wrapped in swaddling clothes and lying in a manger."
★Hail Mary...

12★
O My Jesus, forgive us our sins, save us from the fires of hell; lead all souls to heaven, especially those who are in most need of Thy mercy.
★Amen.

8★
The Angel said, "Glory to God in the highest, and on earth peace to those to whom his favor rests."
★Hail Mary...

11★
Glory be to the Father, and to the Son and to the Holy Spirit.
★As it was in the beginning, is now, and ever shall be, world without end.
★Amen.

9★
The shepherds returned, glorifying and praising God for all they had heard and seen.
★Hail Mary...

10★
Mary kept all these things, reflecting on them in her heart.
★Hail Mary...

THE JOYFUL MYSTERIES
Monday & Saturday

★

4th Joyful Mystery

Mary and Joseph Presented Jesus in the Temple of Jerusalem

★ *Our Father...*

5★
The Magi from the East arrived in Jerusalem. They saw God's star and followed this.
★Hail Mary...

4★
Simeon said to Mary, a sword will pierce your heart.
★Hail Mary...

3★
Simeon blessed them and said to Mary, "This child is destined of the fall and rise of many in Israel."
★Hail Mary...

1★
According to the Law of Moses, every firstborn male shall be consecrated to the Lord.
★Hail Mary...

2★
Simeon said, "For my eyes have seen your salvation, which you prepared in sight of all the people."
★Hail Mary...

6★
The Magi asked, "Where is the newborn king of the Jews? We saw his star at its rising and have come to do Him homage."
★Hail Mary...

7★
The Magi offered gifts to the Divine Child: gold, frankincense and myrrh.
★Hail Mary...

12★
O My Jesus, forgive us our sins, save us from the fires of hell; lead all souls to heaven, especially those who are in most need of Thy mercy.
★Amen.

8★
The Angel appeared to Joseph in a dream and said,"Herod is going to search for the child to destroy Him."
★Hail Mary...

11★
Glory be to the Father, and to the Son and to the Holy Spirit.
★As it was in the beginning, is now, and ever shall be, world without end.
★Amen.

9★
Joseph rose and took the child and His mother, by night and departed for Egypt.
★Hail Mary...

10★
Joseph, Mary and Jesus were living in Nazareth. 'He shall be called a Nazorean.'
★Hail Mary...

THE JOYFUL MYSTERIES
Monday & Saturday

★

5th Joyful Mystery

Mary and Joseph Found Jesus in the Temple

★Our Father...

5★ They were in Jerusalem for the feast of Passover; when Jesus was twelve years old.
★Hail Mary...

4★ Jesus obeyed God in everything and also to Mary and Joseph.
★Hail Mary...

3★ Jesus worked with Joseph as a carpenter.
★Hail Mary...

1★ The Divine Child Jesus.

The grace of God was upon Him.
★Hail Mary...

2★ The child grew and became strong. He was full of wisdom.
★Hail Mary...

6 ★

Mary and Joseph thought that Jesus was in the caravan. However, He wasn't there. After searching for Him, they returned to Jerusalem.
★Hail Mary...

7 ★

After three days they found Him in the Temple, sitting in the midst of the teachers, listening to them and asking them questions.
★Hail Mary...

12 ★

O My Jesus, forgive us our sins, save us from the fires of hell; lead all souls to heaven, especially those who are in most need of Thy mercy.
★Amen.

11 ★

Glory be to the Father, and to the Son and to the Holy Spirit.
★As it was in the beginning, is now, and ever shall be, world without end.
★Amen.

8 ★

All who heard Him were astounded at His understanding and His answers.
★Hail Mary...

9 ★

His mother said to Him, "Son, why have you done this to us? Your father and I have been looking for You with great anxiety."
★Hail Mary...

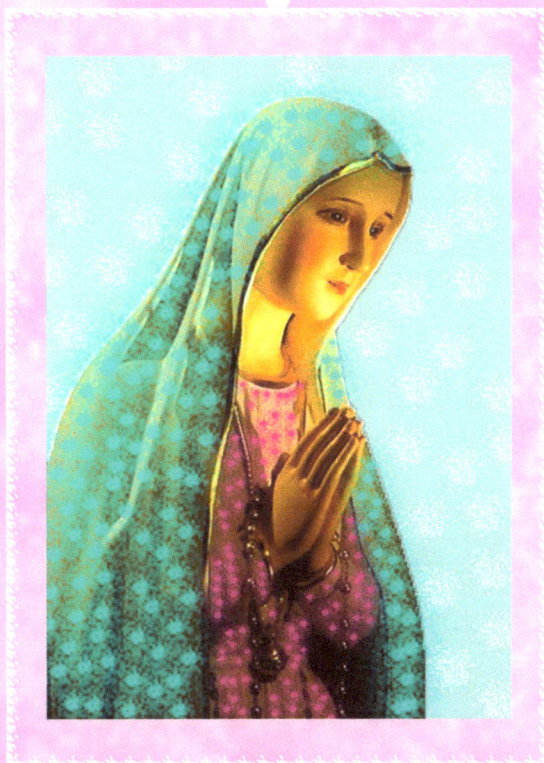

10 ★

Jesus said to them, "Why were you looking for me? Did you not know that I must be in my Father's house?"
★Hail Mary...

THE LUMINOUS MYSTERIES
Thursday

★

1st Luminous Mystery

The Baptism of Jesus at the Jordan River

★ *Our Father...*

5★
He will baptize you with the Holy Spirit and Fire.
★ *Hail Mary...*

4★
"I am baptizing you with water, but one mightier than I is coming."
★*Hail Mary...*

3★
John proclaimed "Repent for the Kingdom of Heaven is at hand!"
★*Hail Mary...*

1★
His name is John, "What will this child be?" For surely the hand of the Lord was with him.
★*Hail Mary...*

2★
John will be called prophet of the Most High, for you will go before the Lord.
★ *Hail Mary...*

6★
Jesus was at the Jordan River to be baptized by him. John said to Jesus, "I need to be baptized by You."
★*Hail Mary...*

7★
Jesus replied "Allow it now, for thus it is fitting for us to fulfill all righteousness"
★*Hail Mary...*

12★
O My Jesus, forgive us our sins, save us from the fires of hell; lead all souls to heaven, especially those who are in most need of Thy mercy.
★*Amen.*

8★
After Jesus was baptized, He came up from the water and behold, the Heavens were opened for Him.
★*Hail Mary...*

11★
Glory be to the Father, and to the Son and to the Holy Spirit.
★*As it was in the beginning, is now, and ever shall be, world without end.*
★*Amen.*

9★
Jesus saw the Spirit of God descending like a dove coming upon Him.
★*Hail Mary...*

10★
A voice came from Heavens, saying, "This is my beloved Son, with whom I am well pleased."
★*Hail Mary...*

THE LUMINOUS MYSTERIES
Thursday

★

2nd Luminous Mystery

Jesus Revealed 'The Messiah' in the Wedding at Cana

★*Our Father...*

5★ Jesus replied, "Woman, my hour has not yet come." ★*Hail Mary...*

4★ The wine ran short. Mary said to Jesus, "They have no wine." ★*Hail Mary...*

3★ Jesus and His disciples were also invited to the wedding. ★*Hail Mary...*

1★ The wedding at Cana, in Galilee. ★*Hail Mary...*

2★ Mary the mother of Jesus was there. ★*Hail Mary...*

6★
Mary said to the servers, "Do whatever He tells you."
★ *Hail Mary...*

7★
Jesus told them "Fill the jars with water."
★*Hail Mary...*

12★
O My Jesus, forgive us our sins, save us from the fires of hell; lead all souls to heaven, especially those who are in most need of Thy mercy.
★*Amen.*

8 ★
Jesus said to them, "Draw some out now and take it to the headwaiter."
★*Hail Mary...*

11★
Glory be to the Father, and to the Son and to the Holy Spirit.
★*As it was in the beginning, is now, and ever shall be, world without end.*
★*Amen.*

9★
The headwaiter said, "Everyone serves good wine first, but you have kept the good wine until now."
★*Hail Mary...*

10★
Jesus revealed His glory, and His disciples began to believe in Him.
★*Hail Mary...*

THE LUMINOUS MYSTERIES
Thursday

★

3rd Luminous Mystery

The Proclamation
God's Kingdom, and
the Call to Conversion

★*Our Father...*

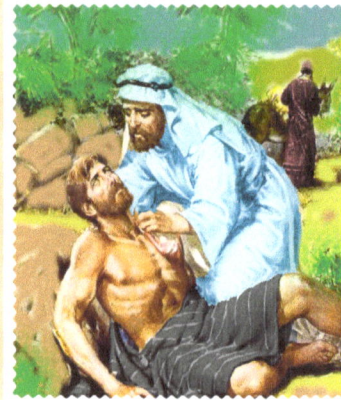

5★ The Good Samaritan was moved with compassion. He took the victim to an inn and cared for him.
★*Hail Mary...*

4★ You shall love the Lord, your God, with all your heart, being, strength and mind, Love your neighbor as yourself.
★*Hail Mary...*

3★ The poor man Lazarus died; he was carried away by angels to heaven. And the rich man also died and was buried.
★*Hail Mary...*

1★ The Sermon on the Mount, 'The Beatitudes' "Blessed are the clean of heart, for they will see God."
★*Hail Mary...*

2★ The Parable of the Sower. Some seeds fell on rich soil, and produced enough good fruit.
★*Hail Mary...*

6 ★
Jesus told to the rich young man, "If you want to enter eternal life, obey the commandments and sell what you have and give to the poor."
★*Hail Mary...*

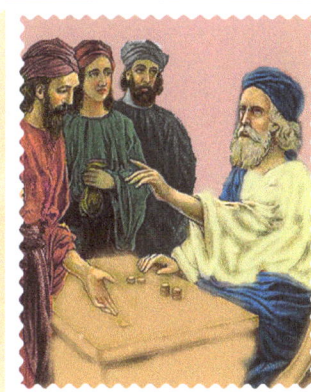

7 ★
The Talents' Parable. Since you were faithful in small matters, I will give you great responsibilities. Come; share your Master's joy.
★*Hail Mary...*

12 ★
O My Jesus, forgive us our sins, save us from the fires of hell; lead all souls to heaven, especially those who are in most need of Thy mercy.
★*Amen.*

8 ★
The Lost Sheep's Parable. It is not the will of your heavenly Father that one of these little ones be lost.
★*Hail Mary...*

11 ★
Glory be to the Father, and to the Son and to the Holy Spirit.
★*As it was in the beginning, is now, and ever shall be, world without end.*
★*Amen.*

9 ★
The kingdom of heaven is like a mustard seed that a person took and sowed in a field.
★*Hail Mary...*

10 ★
Jesus said, "Let the children come to me, and don't prevent them; for the kingdom of heaven belongs to such as these."
★*Hail Mary...*

THE LUMINOUS MYSTERIES
Thursday

★

4th Luminous Mystery

When Jesus Was Transfigured, Moses and Elijah Appeared to Him

★Our Father...

5★
Jesus took the five loaves and two fish, and He said a blessing, broke the loaves, and gave them to the disciples, who in turn gave them to the crowds.
★Hail Mary...

4★
Jesus cleansing of the Temple "Take these out of here, and stop making my Father's house a marketplace."
★Hail Mary...

3★
Jesus has raised Lazarus and other people from the dead. "Who lives and believes in me will never die."
★Hail Mary...

1★
Jesus chose His First Disciples, 'The twelve Apostles'. He said to them, "Follow Me"
★Hail Mary...

2★
Jesus expelled demons, and healed every disease.
★Hail Mary...

6★
Jesus calmed the storm at sea. He did many miracles and everyone believed in Him.
★*Hail Mary...*

7★
Jesus was transfigured before John, James and Peter, on a high mountain.
★*Hail Mary...*

12★
O My Jesus, forgive us our sins, save us from the fires of hell; lead all souls to heaven, especially those who are in most need of Thy mercy.
★*Amen.*

8★
Jesus' face shined like the sun and His clothes became white as light; Moses and Elijah appeared and told to Him.
★*Hail Mary...*

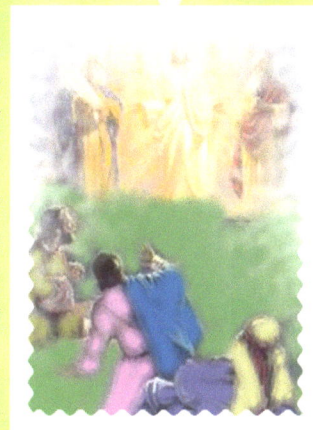

11★
Glory be to the Father, and to the Son and to the Holy Spirit.
★*As it was in the beginning, is now, and ever shall be, world without end.*
★*Amen.*

9★
Peter said to Jesus, "I will make three tents here, one for You, one for Moses and one for Elijah."
★*Hail Mary...*

10★
From the cloud came a voice that said, "This is my beloved Son, with whom I am well pleased; listen to Him."
★*Hail Mary...*

THE LUMINOUS MYSTERIES
Thursday

★

5th Luminous Mystery

The Institution of the Holy Eucharist

★Our Father...

5★
The Lamb of God, who takes away the sin of the world.
★Hail Mary...

4★
This is my body, which will be given for you; do this in memory of me.
★Hail Mary...

3★
This is my blood of the covenant, which will be shed on behalf of many for the forgiveness of sins.
★Hail Mary...

1★
The Last Supper. Jesus said to the Apostles, "I have eagerly desired to eat this Passover with you before I suffer".
★Hail Mary...

2★
Jesus took the bread, said the blessing, broke it, and gave it to the Apostles.
★Hail Mary...

6 ★
The Holy Mass, Glorify the Father, we offer Christ's body, blood, soul and Divinity for the forgiveness our sins and those of the entire world.
★ Hail Mary...

7 ★
The Holy Eucharist contains entire spiritual wealth: Christ himself, our Passover and living bread. "Do this in remembrance of me"
★ Hail Mary...

12 ★
O My Jesus, forgive us our sins, save us from the fires of hell; lead all souls to heaven, especially those who are in most need of Thy mercy.
★ Amen.

11 ★
Glory be to the Father, and to the Son and to the Holy Spirit.
★ As it was in the beginning, is now, and ever shall be, world without end.
★ Amen.

8 ★
The sacrament of Reconciliation for the conversion of sins.
★ Hail Mary...

9 ★
Lord, I am not worthy that you should enter under my roof , but only say the word and my soul shall be healed.
★ Hail Mary...

10 ★
Lord present in the Tabernacle. Blessed and praised, adored forever be the Blessed Sacrament.
★ Hail Mary...

THE SORROWFUL MYSTERIES
Tuesday & Friday

★

1st Sorrowful Mystery

The Agony of Jesus in the Mount of Olives

★ Our Father...

5 ★
Jesus said, "Where I go you cannot come," "If you are my disciples, Love one another."
★ Hail Mary...

4 ★
Jesus said to his disciples, "I say to you, one of you will betray me."
★ Hail Mary...

3 ★
Jesus washes the disciples' feet. He said to Peter, "Unless I wash you, you will have no inheritance with me."
★ Hail Mary...

1 ★
Blessed is he who comes in the name of the Lord; Hosanna in the Highest.
★ Hail Mary...

2 ★
She has anticipated anointing my body for burial.
★ Hail Mary...

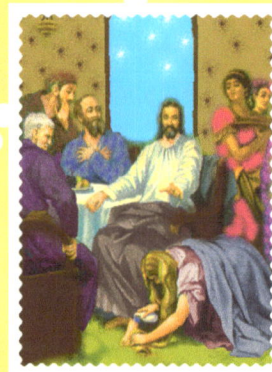

6 ★
Jesus prayed to God, "My Father, if it is possible, let this cup pass from me, yet, not as I will, but as you will."
★*Hail Mary...*

7 ★
An Angel appeared to Jesus that comforted Him. He was in such agony and He prayed so fervently.
★*Hail Mary...*

12 ★
O My Jesus, forgive us our sins, save us from the fires of hell; lead all souls to heaven, especially those who are in most need of Thy mercy.
★*Amen.*

8 ★
Jesus said to Peter, "So you could not keep watch with me? Watch and pray that you may not undergo the test. "
★*Hail Mary...*

11 ★
Glory be to the Father, and to the Son and to the Holy Spirit.
★*As it was in the beginning, is now, and ever shall be, world without end.*
★*Amen.*

9 ★
Judas Iscariot had given them a sign, "The man I shall kiss is the one; arrest Him."
★*Hail Mary...*

10 ★
Jesus said, "Put your sword back into its sheath, for all who take the sword will perish by the sword."
★*Hail Mary...*

THE SORROWFUL MYSTERIES
Tuesday & Friday

★

2nd Sorrowful Mystery

The Scourging of Jesus at the Pillar

★Our Father...

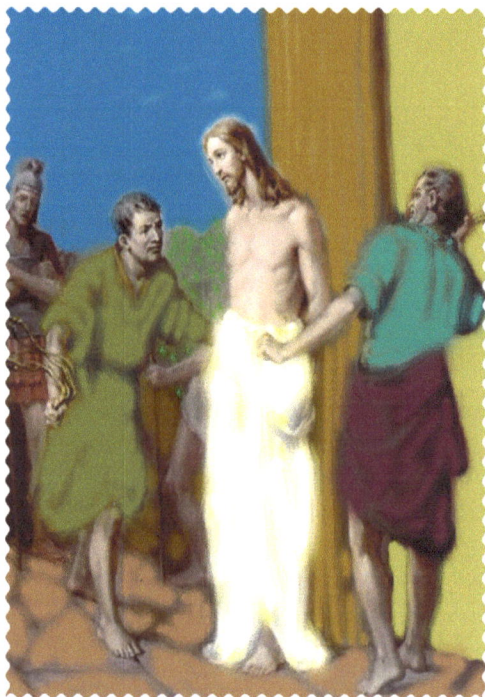

5★ *Jesus was brought before Pilate, who asked Him, "Are you the King of the Jews?"*
★*Hail Mary...*

4★ *Jesus said to Peter, "Before the cock crows you will deny me three times." He went out and began to weep bitterly.*
★*Hail Mary...*

3★ *Peter denies Jesus, "I do not know that man."*
★*Hail Mary...*

1★ *From now on you will see the Son of Man seated at the right hand of the Power and coming on the clouds of Heaven.*
★*Hail Mary...*

2★ *They spit in the face and slapped Him.*
★*Hail Mary...*

6★
Herod asked Jesus
many questions,
but Jesus did not
answer him.
★*Hail Mary...*

7★
Pilate asked to the
crowd, "Do you want
me to release to you
the king of the Jews?"
They cried out again,
"Not this one but
Barabbas!"
★*Hail Mary...*

12★
O My Jesus,
forgive us our sins,
save us from the fires of hell;
lead all souls to heaven,
especially those who are in
most need of Thy mercy.
★*Amen.*

8★
Pilate freed
Barabbas and
sentenced
Jesus to
death.
★*Hail Mary...*

11★
Glory be to the Father,
and to the Son
and to the Holy Spirit.
★*As it was in the beginning,
is now, and ever shall be,
world without end.*
★*Amen.*

9★
Pontius
Pilate
had Jesus
scourged.
★*Hail Mary...*

10★
The soldiers
beat and
mocked Jesus.
★*Hail Mary...*

THE SORROWFUL MYSTERIES
Tuesday & Friday

★

3rd Sorrowful Mystery

The Crowning
of Thorns

★Our Father...

5★
They put a reed
in His right hand.
★ Hail Mary...

4★
The soldiers
stripped off
His clothes,
then dressed
Him in a
purple cloak.
★Hail Mary...

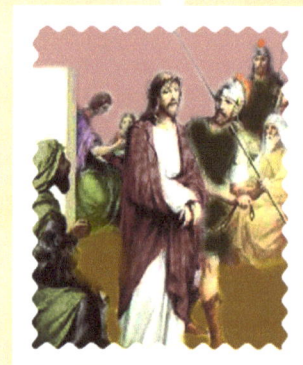

3★
The soldiers
took Jesus
inside the
praetorium.
★Hail Mary...

1★
The soldiers had
made a crown out
of thorns.
★Hail Mary...

2★
They put the
crown of thorns
on His head.
★Hail Mary...

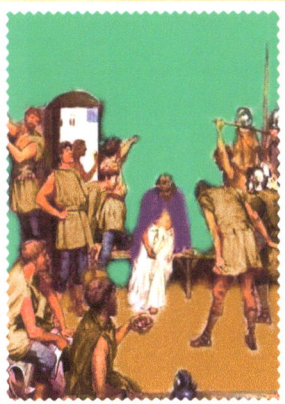

6★
The soldiers knelt before Him, laughed, saying, "Hail, King of the Jews!"
★*Hail Mary...*

7★
They spat upon Him and took the reed and struck Him on the head.
★*Hail Mary...*

12★
O My Jesus, forgive us our sins, save us from the fires of hell; lead all souls to heaven, especially those who are in most need of Thy mercy.
★*Amen.*

8★
His silence and humility, was stronger than pain.
★*Hail Mary...*

11★
Glory be to the Father, and to the Son and to the Holy Spirit.
★*As it was in the beginning, is now, and ever shall be, world without end.*
★*Amen.*

9★
They stripped Him of the cloak, dressed Him back into His own clothes.
★*Hail Mary...*

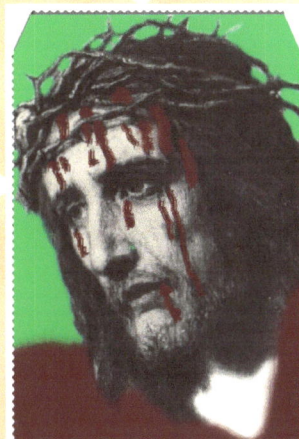

10★
His pain was deep, but what really broke His heart was witnessing so much human wickedness and evil.
★*Hail Mary...*

THE SORROWFUL MYSTERIES
Tuesday & Friday

★

4th Sorrowful Mystery

Jesus Carried His Cross all the Way at Golgotha

★*Our Father...*

5★
Jesus fell the second time.
★*Hail Mary...*

4★
Simon of Cyrene helped Jesus to carry the cross.
★*Hail Mary...*

3★
Jesus met His Blessed Mother Mary.
★*Hail Mary...*

1★
Jesus was condemned to death, and was forced to carry His cross.
★*Hail Mary...*

2★
Jesus fell the first time..
★*Hail Mary...*

6★
Veronica wiped the face of Jesus.
★*Hail Mary...*

7★
Jesus met the women of Jerusalem and comforted them.
★*Hail Mary...*

12★
O My Jesus, forgive us our sins, save us from the fires of hell; lead all souls to heaven, especially those who are in most need of Thy mercy.
★*Amen.*

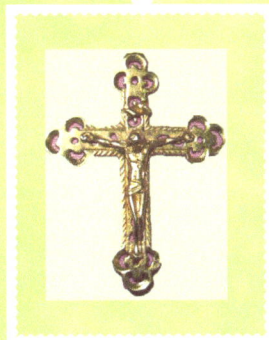

8★
Jesus fell a third time.
★*Hail Mary...*

11★
Glory be to the Father, and to the Son and to the Holy Spirit.
★*As it was in the beginning, is now, and ever shall be, world without end.*
★*Amen.*

10★
Jesus said, "Father, forgive them, they know not what they do."
★*Hail Mary...*

10★
Jesus was stripped of His garments.
★*Hail Mary...*

THE SORROWFUL MYSTERIES
Tuesday & Friday

★

5th Sorrowful Mystery

The Crucifixion and Death of Our Lord Jesus Christ

★*Our Father...*

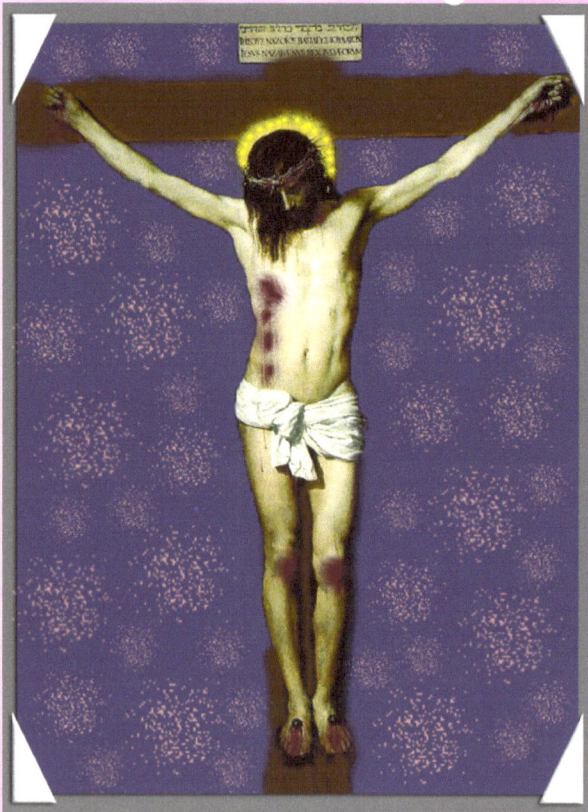

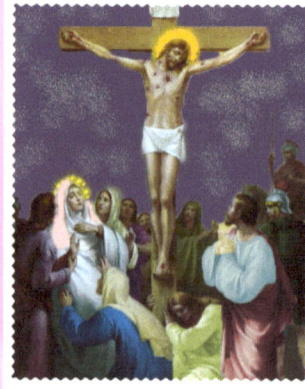

5★
Jesus said to His mother, "Woman, behold, your son." And He said to John, "Behold, your mother"
★*Hail Mary...*

4★
Jesus replied to the criminal, "Amen, I say to you, today you will be with me in Paradise."
★*Hail Mary...*

3★
The passage of scripture said, "They divided my garments among them, and for my vesture they cast lots."
★*Hail Mary...*

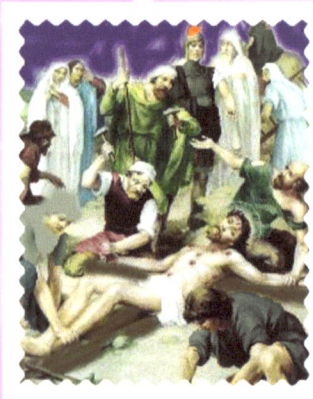

1★
The Soldiers had crucified Jesus. They nailed Jesus to the cross.
★*Hail Mary...*

2★
On his head they placed a sign that said, 'This is the king of the Jews'.
★*Hail Mary...*

6★
Jesus exclaimed,
"Father, into your
hands I commend
my spirit!"
★Hail Mary...

7★
Jesus cried out
in a loud voice,
"My God, my God,
why have you
forsaken me?"
★Hail Mary...

12★
O My Jesus,
forgive us our sins,
save us from the fires of hell;
lead all souls to heaven,
especially those who are in
most need of Thy mercy.
★Amen.

8★
Jesus said,
"I thirst."
When He had
received the
wine, He said,
"It is finished."
★Hail Mary...

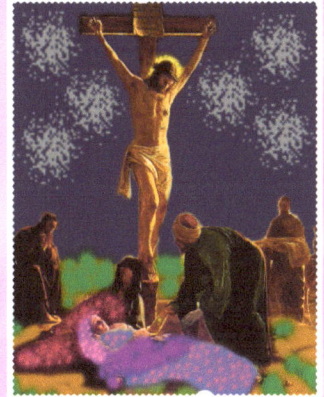

11★
Glory be to the Father,
and to the Son
and to the Holy Spirit.
★As it was in the beginning,
is now, and ever shall be,
world without end.
★Amen.

9★
One soldier
thrust his
lance into
His side, and
immediately
blood and
water
flowed out.
★Hail Mary...

10★
Mary embraced
Jesus's dead body
in her arms after
He was brought
down from the
cross.
Lord, Have Mercy.
★Hail Mary...

THE GLORIOUS MYSTERIES
Wednesday & Sunday

★

1st Glorious Mystery

The Resurrection of Our Lord Jesus Christ

★*Our Father...*

5★
Soldiers sealed the tomb by affixing a seal on the stone and stood guard outside.
★*Hail Mary...*

4★
They laid Jesus in a new tomb located in the garden that He was crucified in.
★*Hail Mary...*

3★
They bound Him with burial cloths along with the spices, according to the Jewish burial custom.
★*Hail Mary...*

1★
Joseph of Arimathea asked Pilate if he could remove the body of Jesus.
★*Hail Mary...*

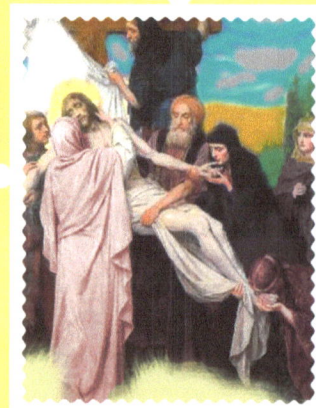

2★
Joseph and Nicodemus had taken down the body of Jesus from the cross.
★*Hail Mary...*

6★
The women found the tomb open, an Angel from the heaven told them, "Do not be afraid!"
★*Hail Mary...*

7★
The angel said to the women, "He is not here, for He has been raised just as He said."
★*Hail Mary...*

12★
O My Jesus, forgive us our sins, save us from the fires of hell; lead all souls to heaven, especially those who are in most need of Thy mercy.
★*Amen.*

8★
Jesus appeared to Mary Magdalene. "I am going to my Father and your Father, to my God and your God".
★*Hail Mary...*

11★
Glory be to the Father, and to the Son and to the Holy Spirit. As it was in the beginning, is now, and ever shall be, world without end.
★*Amen.*

9★
Jesus appeared to two disciples, "As the Father has sent me, so I send you." "Receive the Holy Spirit."
★*Hail Mary...*

10★
Jesus appeared to His apostles, "Peace be with you."
★*Hail Mary...*

THE GLORIOUS MYSTERIES
Wednesday & Sunday

★

2nd Glorious Mystery

The Ascension of Lord Jesus Christ to Heaven

★Our Father...

5★ You will be my witnesses in Jerusalem, throughout Judea and Samaria, and to the ends of the earth.
★Hail Mary...

4★ John baptized with water, but you will be baptized with the Holy Spirit.
★Hail Mary...

3★ He spoke about the kingdom of God. Jesus is the Messiah, the Son of God, and that through this belief you may have life in His name.
★Hail Mary...

1★ Jesus rose from the dead. "Blessed are those who have not seen and have believed."
★Hail Mary...

2★ Jesus was appearing several times to His disciples.
★Hail Mary...

6 ★
They were looking on and Jesus was lifted up, and a cloud took Him from their sight.
★*Hail Mary...*

7 ★
He will return in the same way as you have seen Him going into Heaven.
★*Hail Mary...*

12 ★
O My Jesus, forgive us our sins, save us from the fires of hell; lead all souls to heaven, especially those who are in most need of Thy mercy.
★*Amen.*

8 ★
Jesus Christ ascended into Heaven.
★*Hail Mary...*

11 ★
Glory be to the Father, and to the Son and to the Holy Spirit.
★*As it was in the beginning, is now, and ever shall be, world without end.*
★*Amen.*

9 ★
Jesus Christ is seated at the right hand of God the Father Almighty.
★*Hail Mary...*

10 ★
Jesus will come again in glory to judge the living and the dead, and His kingdom will have no end.
★*Hail Mary...*

THE GLORIOUS MYSTERIES
Wednesday & Sunday

★

3rd Glorious Mystery

The Holy Spirit, Descent Upon the Apostles and Disciples.

★ Our Father...

5★ John was the Beloved Disciple.

Peter, Jesus said to him, "Upon this rock I will build my Church. I will give you the keys to the Kingdom of Heaven."
★ Hail Mary...

4★ They were all filled with the Holy Spirit and began to speak in different languages.
★ Hail Mary...

3★ There appeared to them tongues of fire, to rest on each one of them.
★ Hail Mary...

1★ The Apostles prayed for a new apostle, they proposed Barsabbas and Matthias. Matthias was chosen.
★ Hail Mary...

2★ The Apostles, Disciples and the Blessed Virgin Mary were in one place together.
★ Hail Mary...

6★
Philip told Jesus "Show us the Father."

Bartholomew (Nathanael), said to Jesus, "Master, You are the Son of God; You are the King of Israel".
★Hail Mary...

7★
Matthew: Levi, the tax collector, witnessed the Resurrection and the Ascension.

James the Greater witnessed the transfiguration and the agony.
★Hail Mary...

12★
O My Jesus,
forgive us our sins,
save us from the fires of hell;
lead all souls to heaven,
especially those who are in
most need of Thy mercy.
★Amen.

8★
James, son of Alpheus was called, 'The Younger James'

Jude Thaddeus was faithful servant and friend of Jesus.
★Hail Mary...

11★
Glory be to the Father,
and to the Son
and to the Holy Spirit.
★As it was in the beginning,
is now, and ever shall be,
world without end.
★Amen.

9★
Andrew told his brother Simon Peter, "We have found the Messiah"

Matthias was chosen by the eleven Apostles.
★Hail Mary...

10★
Simon was called, 'Zealot or Canaanite'.

Thomas, the twin said, "Let us also die with Him."
★Hail Mary...

THE GLORIOUS MYSTERIES
Wednesday & Sunday

5 ★
Mary had profound humility and was prudent. She always accepted the will of God the Father in her life.
★ *Hail Mary...*

★

4th Glorious Mystery

The Assumption of the Blessed Virgin Mary in Body and Soul in to Heaven

★ *Our Father...*

4 ★
Mary spent her life praying, understanding, loving and trusting in God.
★ *Hail Mary...*

3 ★
Mary has been a model of all moral virtues, among them are: faith, charity, hope and obedience.
★ *Hail Mary...*

1 ★
Since Mary was little she was surrounded by love, light, and wisdom.
★ *Hail Mary...*

2 ★
Mary was kind to everyone and specially to the poor people, and she never offended her parents.
★ *Hail Mary...*

6★
God found in the Virgin Mary a beautiful purity and great virtues, that made her the perfect mother of His beloved Son.
★*Hail Mary...*

7★
Mary was the mother and a disciple of Jesus. She meditated on the things of her son, Jesus.
★*Hail Mary...*

12★
O My Jesus, forgive us our sins, save us from the fires of hell; lead all souls to heaven, especially those who are in most need of Thy mercy.
★*Amen.*

8★
The Virgin Mary suffered pain when her son died, as if a sword pierced her heart."
★*Hail Mary...*

11★
Glory be to the Father, and to the Son and to the Holy Spirit.
★*As it was in the beginning, is now, and ever shall be, world without end.*
★*Amen.*

9★
The Blessed Virgin Mary ascended into heaven, 'Rejoice' because with Christ she reigns forever.
★*Hail Mary...*

10★
From now on call me 'Blessed' all generations, because the Almighty has done great things for me.
★*Hail Mary...*

THE GLORIOUS MYSTERIES
Wednesday & Sunday

★

5th Glorious Mystery

The Crowning of the Blessed Mother Virgin Mary, as Queen of Heaven and Earth

★Our Father...

5★ Mary is our intercessor to her beloved son Jesus.
★ Hail Mary...

4★ Mary was crowned "QUEEN of the UNIVERSE" by her grace and by divine relationship.
★Hail Mary...

3★ Mary has been model of all Catholics throughout her entire life and has given faithfulness, patience and respect to the things of God.
★ Hail Mary...

1★ Mary followed the teachings of her parents and the chief priests.
★ Hail Mary...

2★ Mary always felt the presence of the Spirit of God in her life.
★Hail Mary...

6★
Our Lady of Fatima said, "Pray the Rosary every day, do penance and acts of reparation, and make sacrifices to save sinners".
★Hail Mary...

7★
Our Lady of Lourdes taught us how prayer should be about praise, gratitude, trust joy, suffering, serenity, solitude health and illness.
★Hail Mary...

12★
O My Jesus, forgive us our sins, save us from the fires of hell; lead all souls to heaven, especially those who are in most need of Thy mercy.
★Amen.

8★
Virgin of Guadalupe, declared herself to be the Virgin Mary, the mother of Jesus Christ. Confide in her.
★Hail Mary...

11★
Glory be to the Father, and to the Son and to the Holy Spirit.
★As it was in the beginning, is now, and ever shall be, world without end.
★Amen.

9★
Our Lady of the Miraculous Medal, whoever wears this receives great graces, and protection.
★Hail Mary...

10★
The Blessed Virgin Mary has appeared in different places, leaving messages like, pray to God for sinners, have Faith, love God, and one another".
★Hail Mary...

HAIL, HOLY QUEEN

★

1 ★
*Hail, holy Queen
mother of mercy,
our life, our
sweetness, and
our hope.*

2 ★
*To thee do we
cry, poor banished
children of Eve,*

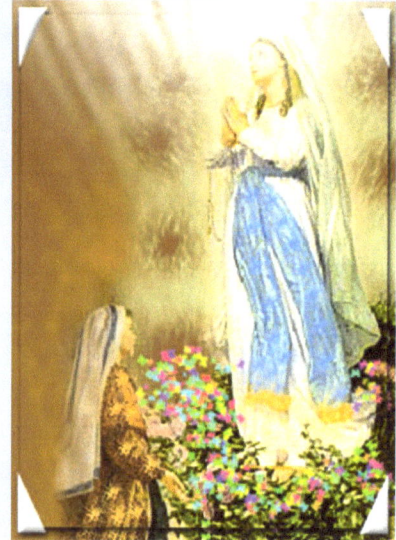

3 ★
*To thee do we
send up our sighs
mourning and weeping
in this valley of tears.*

4 ★
*Turn then, most gracious
advocate, thine eyes of
mercy toward us,*

5 ★

*and after this our exile
show us the blessed
fruit of thy womb,
Jesus.*

6 ★

*O clement,
O loving,
O sweet
Virgin Mary.*

7 ★

*Pray for us,
O Holy Mother
of God.*

8 ★

*That we may be made
worthy of the
Promises of Christ*
★*Amen.*

FOR THE INTENTIONS OF THE HOLY FATHER

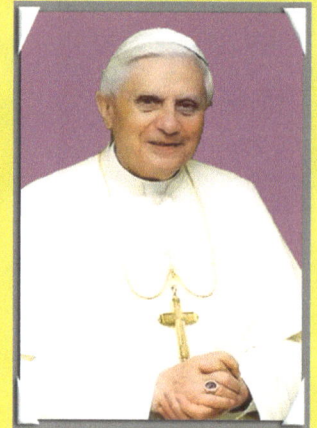

1

Our Father, who art in heaven,
Hallowed be Thy Name;
thy Kingdom come;
thy will be done on earth
as it is in heaven.

Give us this day our daily bread;
and forgive us our trespasses,
as we forgive those who trespass
against us; and lead us not into
temptation, but deliver us
from evil.
Amen.

2
(3 Hail Marys)
Hail, Mary full of Grace,
the Lord is with thee.Blessed
art thou among women, and
blessed is the fruit of thy womb,
Jesus

Holy Mary,Mother of God,
pray for us sinners now,
and at the hour of death.
Amen.

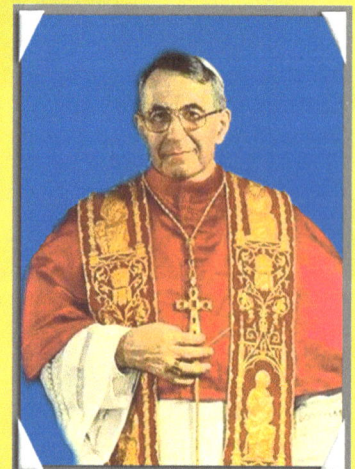

3

Glory be to the Father, and to
the Son and to the Holy Spirit.

As it was in the beginning,
is now, and ever shall be,
world without end.
Amen.

CHAPLET OF THE DIVINE MERCY

JESUS I TRUST IN YOU

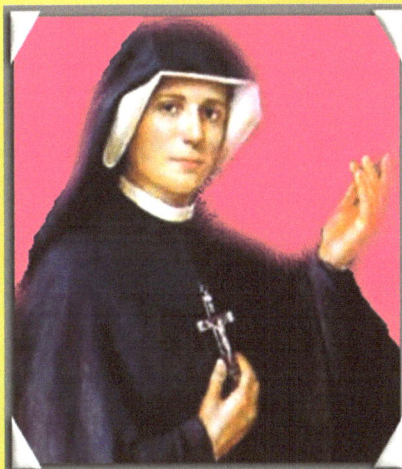

1★
Eternal Father,
I offer you the Body and Blood,
Soul and Divinity of Your dearly
beloved Son,

Our Lord Jesus Christ, in
atonement for our sins and
those of the whole world

2★
For the sake of
His sorrowful Passion,

have mercy on us and
on the whole world
(say three times)

3★
Holy God,
Holy Mighty One,
Holy Immortal One,
have mercy on us and
on the whole world.
★*Amen.*

HOLY SOULS

1 ★

*Lord Jesus Christ
we pray for the holy souls
in purgatory so they release
their pain and sorrow, and
thus be purified and radiate
your light and love.*

*After this, they may enjoy
the wonderful encounter
with God Almighty.*

2 ★

Eternal rest gives unto them,

★*O Lord, and let perpetual light
shine upon them.*
(Repeat three times)
★*Amen.*

★SAINT MICHAEL THE ARCHANGEL

*St. Michael the Archangel, defend us
in battle. Be our defense against the
wickedness and snares of the Devil.*

*May God rebuke him we humbly pray,
and do thou, O Prince of the heavenly
hosts, by the power of God, thrust into
hell Satan, and all the evil spirits,
who prowl about the world
seeking the ruin of souls.*
★*Amen.*

★ THE ANIMA CHRISTI

1 ★
Soul of Christ, *sanctify me*

Body of Christ, *save me*

Blood of Christ, *inebriate me*

Water from Christ's side, *wash me*

2 ★
Passion of Christ, *Strengthen me*

O good Jesus, *hear me*

Within Thy wounds, *hide me*

3 ★
Suffer me not to be separated from Thee
From the malicious enemy, *defend me*

In the hour of my death, *call me*
And bid me come unto Thee

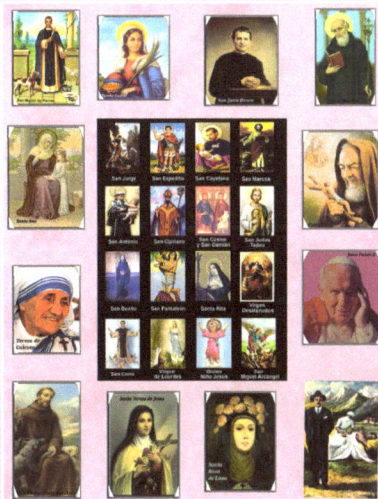

4 ★
That I may praise
Thee with Thy saints
and with Thy angels
Forever and ever
★ *Amen.*

MEMORARE

★

Remember,
O most gracious Virgin Mary,
that never was it known that
anyone who fled to thy protection,
implored thy help, or sought thine
intercession was left unaided.

Inspired by this confidence, I
fly unto thee, O Virgin of virgins,
my mother; to thee do I come,
before thee I stand, sinful and
sorrowful.

O Mother of the Word Incarnate,
despises not my petitions, but in
thy mercy hear and answer me.
★Amen.

Most Sacred Heart of Jesus,
★have mercy on us.

Inmaculate Heart of Mary,
★ pray for us.

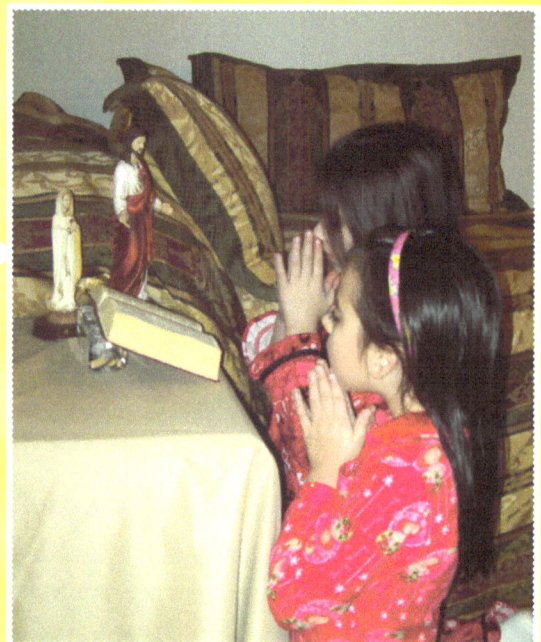

MY GUARDIAN ANGEL

★

1★
Angel of God,
my guardian dear,
To whom God's love
commits me here,

2★
Ever this day,
be at my side,

3★
To light and guard,
Rule and guide.

★*Amen.*

LITANY OF THE BLESSED VIRGIN MARY

1 ★

Lord, have mercy on us.
Christ, have mercy on us.

Lord, have mercy on us.
Christ, have mercy on us.

Christ, hear us.
Christ, graciously hear us.

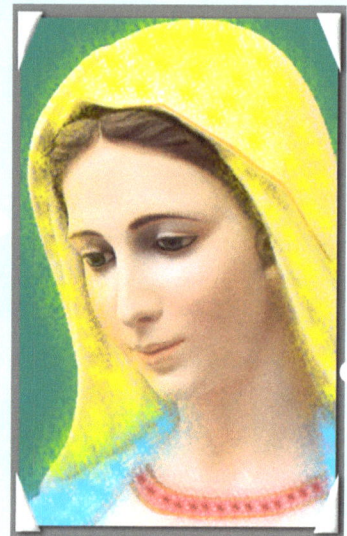

2 ★

God the Father of heaven,
Have mercy on us.

God the Son, Redeemer of the world,
Have mercy on us.

God the Holy Spirit,
Have mercy on us.

Holy Trinity, One God,
Have mercy on us.

3 ⭐

Holy Mary,
pray for us.

Holy Mother of God,
pray for us.

Holy Virgin of virgins,
pray for us.

Mother of Christ.
pray for us.

Mother of the Church,
pray for us.

Mother of divine grace,
pray for us.

4 ⭐

Mother most pure,
pray for us.

Mother most chaste,
pray for us.

Mother inviolate,
pray for us.

Mother undefiled,
pray for us.

Mother most amiable,
pray for us.

5 ★
Mother most admirable,
pray for us.

Mother of good counsel,
pray for us.

Mother of our Creator,
pray for us.

Mother of our Savior,
pray for us.

Virgin most prudent,
pray for us.

6 ★
Virgin most venerable,
pray for us.

Virgin most renowned,
pray for us.

Virgin most powerful,
pray for us.

Virgin most merciful,
pray for us.

Virgin most faithful,
pray for us.

7 ★
Mirror of justice,
pray for us.

Seat of wisdom,
pray for us.

Cause of our joy,
pray for us.

Spiritual vessel,
pray for us.

Vessel of honor,
pray for us.

Singular vessel of
devotion,
pray for us.

8 ★
Mystical rose,
pray for us.

Tower of David,
pray for us.

Tower of ivory,
pray for us.

House of gold,
pray for us.

9 ★
Ark of the covenant,
pray for us.

Gate of heaven,
pray for us.

Morning star,
pray for us.

Health of the sick,
pray for us.

Refuge of sinners,
pray for us.

Comforter of the afflicted.
pray for us.

Help of Christians.
pray for us.

Queen of Angels.
pray for us.

Queen of patriarchs.
pray for us.

Queen of prophets.
pray for us.

Queen of apostles.
pray for us.

Queen of martyrs.
pray for us.

Queen of confessors.
pray for us.

Queen of virgins.
pray for us.

Queen of all saints.
pray for us.

Queen conceived without original sin.
pray for us.

12 ★
*Queen assumed
into heaven,*
pray for us.

*Queen of the most
holy Rosary,*
pray for us.

Queen of families,
pray for us.

Queen of peace,
pray for us.

13 ★
*Lamb of God, who takes
away the sins of the world,*
Spare us, O Lord.

*Lamb of God, who takes
away the sins of the world,*
Graciously hear us, O Lord.

*Lamb of God, who takes
away the sins of the world,*
Have mercy on us.

14 ★
*Pray for us, O holy Mother of God,
That we may be made worthy of
the promises of Christ.*

★*Amen.*

The Sign of the Cross

1★

*In the name
of
the Father*

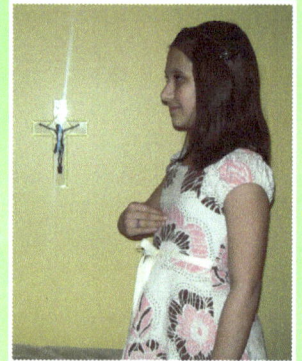

2★

**And of
the Son**

3★

**And of
the Holy**

5★

Amen

4★

Spirit

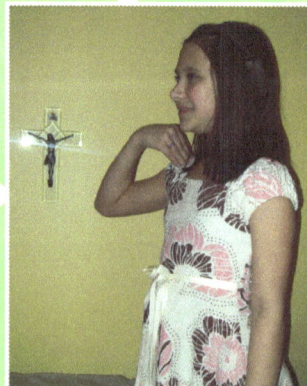

www.ingramcontent.com/pod-product-compliance
Lightning Source LLC
LaVergne TN
LVHW072106070426
835509LV00002B/34